Humphrey

Chapter 1

"Hey, Karl!" Jenna yelled to me from a window in our new house. "Come and look at this."

"What is it?" I asked, standing on the steps with a box of photos in my arms.

Dad had unlocked the door for Jenna while we unloaded everything that Mom didn't trust the movers with. She didn't trust Jenna with those things, either.

"Give the box to me," Dad said, "and find out what Jenna is doing."

I found Jenna in the kitchen, opening and shutting the door of a cat cage.

"A cat cage?" I said. "It must belong to the Johnsons, who just moved out."

"Yes," Jenna agreed. She had a sly look on her face. "But where's the cat?" She stared around the kitchen as though she expected to see it pop out of a cupboard.

"I don't know." I was getting impatient. "They wouldn't have left it behind, that's for sure."

"Look, here's a note," Jenna said.

Dear Valentine Family,

Our cat, Humphrey, is missing. If he comes back, there's food in the pantry for him. We will come to get him in the morning.

Thank you.

The note was signed with a squiggle that I couldn't read.

"Where's the can opener?" Jenna asked as she came out of the pantry with a can of cat food.

"Wouldn't it be a good idea to find the cat first?" I asked.

I felt smart for saying that.

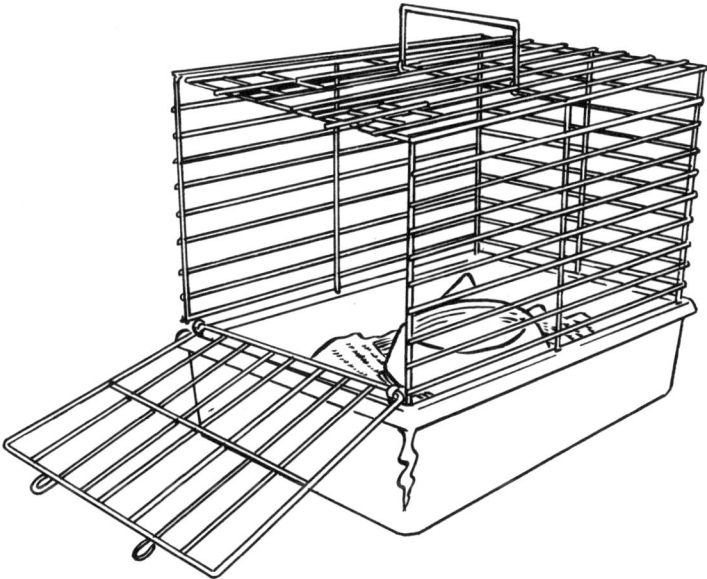

Chapter 2

In the end, it was Humphrey who found *us*. We were sitting at the table, eating dinner, when the door squeaked open.

And in he walked. He was a big, striped cat with a ragged ear and a bent tail.

"Meow," he cried.

"The cat!" Jenna yelled.

"No," I said. "It's a pig."

"Karl," Dad said with a frown, "don't tease your sister. And Jenna, keep quiet or you'll scare the cat."

But it was going to take much more than just Jenna yelling to scare Humphrey.

He strolled across the kitchen floor and rubbed his furry head against everyone's legs.

After everyone had eaten, including Humphrey, he curled up between Jenna and me while we watched television. He purred and blinked his yellow eyes when we petted him.

"It's bedtime, Jenna," Mom called.

"I'll take Humphrey," Jenna said. "He can sleep on my bed."

"No," replied Mom. "It's better if he goes outside tonight."

"Oh, Mom," begged Jenna.

"I'll tell you what," I suggested. "I'll open a window in case he wants to go out during the night."

Later that night, Humphrey did leave Jenna's room, but he only went as far as my room. He slept on my bed and was still there when Mrs. Johnson came to get him the next morning.

Jenna started to cry. I didn't feel good about him leaving, either.

Mrs. Johnson said kindly, "You don't want a big, old cat with a ragged ear and bent tail. Why don't you ask your mother for a kitten?"

Jenna shook her head.

"Cheer up, Jenna," said Mom. "Let's all go find Humphrey."

So, we began our search. We looked inside and outside and inside again, under Jenna's bed, over the neighbor's fence, and in the garden shed. But Humphrey wasn't there. He wasn't anywhere.

"I'll come back this weekend," Mrs. Johnson said. "I'm so sorry."

Jenna and I weren't sorry. We couldn't help smiling, especially when Humphrey meowed at us from the rooftop.

Chapter 3

Mrs. Johnson called on Saturday morning. "I'll be there in a half hour," she said. "Could you please put Humphrey into his cage?"

"No trouble at all," said Dad. He sounded happy, but I saw him give Humphrey a cuddle before he shut the cage door.

A half hour went by, but Mrs. Johnson still hadn't arrived.

"It won't be much longer now, Humphrey," I said and petted him through the bars with one finger.

Jenna sniffled and rubbed her eyes with her hands.

"Look, Jenna," I said, trying to make her feel better, "he's an old cat. Look at that ragged ear he has from fighting."

"But I like Humphrey's ragged ear," Jenna bawled.

Suddenly, the phone rang. It was Mrs. Johnson again. "Would you please let Humphrey out? My car has a flat tire and I don't have a spare. I'll be at least an hour. I'm so sorry."

Jenna sniffed away her tears and opened the cage while I got a can of cat food. I tipped it into Humphrey's dish, and he quickly ate every bit of it. Then he bumped his head against Jenna's legs while she poured him a small bowl of milk.

Finally, Mrs. Johnson arrived. I ran to the door and tried to stop Humphrey from getting out. But I didn't try too hard. He raced down the steps, across the lawn, and right up to the top of an oak tree. We stood underneath the tree and called his name over and over.

Humphrey meowed back. But he wouldn't come down. He wouldn't even come down when Mom turned on the can opener.

"I'll have to come back on Thursday," Mrs. Johnson sighed. "I'm really sorry about all of this."

Later, when I went into my room to do my homework, I found Humphrey asleep on my bed.

He woke up long enough to meow at me.

Chapter 4

Humphrey patiently waited for us to come home from school every day.

He would follow us up the sidewalk, meowing all the way.

Each night, Jenna and I took turns cuddling him in front of the television. We set the oven timer so we both had the same amount of time with him.

"Don't get too used to him," Dad warned us. "He isn't our cat."

Thursday arrived and we had only one can of cat food left.

Humphrey had just finished eating, when Mom said, "Mrs. Johnson will be here at seven o'clock to pick him up. I'll put him in the garden shed so we can find him."

"I'll carry him," I said.

"No, let me," Jenna argued.

"We'll both do it," I said.

I picked him up, and Jenna held his tail. He purred all the way to the shed.

"No other cat would put up with that," Dad said. "Not for a second."

Mom opened the shed door, and we put him inside.

Suddenly, he stopped purring and crouched on the floor. He stared into the corner and flicked his tail.

"What is it?" Jenna asked. "What does he see?"

"A mouse, I bet," Dad said, peering over our shoulders. "Shut the door and leave him to it."

We left Humphrey in the dark and listened to all the rattling noises that came from the shed.

"What was that noise?" Jenna asked. Her eyes looked like shiny, blue beads.

"Shhhh," said Dad.

We heard a clatter as though the garden rake had come off its hook. Then, everything was quiet.

Dad opened the door, and Humphrey looked out at us. He tried to meow, but the mouse got in the way.

Chapter 5

Mom was pleased with Humphrey for catching the mouse. She was sure it was the same mouse that had been getting into the vegetable seeds in the shed. "You're a good cat," she said and petted him. "But you'll have to stay in the shed until Mrs. Johnson comes for you."

"Good-bye, Humphrey," Jenna whispered. She was trying not to cry. I couldn't say anything.

"Meow," we heard him answer loudly as Mom shut the shed door.

When it was time for Mrs. Johnson to arrive, Jenna came into my room, and I read a story to her.

Jenna and I didn't want to be there when Humphrey went away.

I heard the car drive up, and I started to read louder.

Mrs. Johnson knocked on the front door. I stopped reading. I heard Mom telling her that Humphrey had caught a mouse. Then, I heard the cat cage rattling as Mom carried it out to the shed.

Jenna shook my arm and tapped the book. I went on saying the words, but I wasn't paying attention to what the story was about.

Mom and Mrs. Johnson had been outside for ages. What were they doing? I wondered. It shouldn't take this long to put a cat in a cage.

Then, I remembered how long it had taken for us to catch Humphrey – more than a week. So what was another few minutes?

At last, I saw Mrs. Johnson carrying the cat cage. One shoulder was lower than the other because Humphrey was so heavy. His yellow eyes stared at me through the bars. I saw his mouth open, but I couldn't hear him meow.

I watched Mrs. Johnson open her car door and put him on the back seat. She smiled and waved at me. I waved back, but I didn't feel like smiling.

A moment later, the car disappeared down the road.

Chapter 6

Jenna cried when Mom put her to bed that night. I must have had a funny look on my face, too, because Dad said, "Don't you start crying as well. You knew from the beginning he was the Johnsons' cat." He rattled his newspaper, but I don't think he was reading it.

Thank goodness we had school the next day and Jenna had something else to think about. I hadn't finished my homework, and I knew I was going to be in trouble.

After school, Humphrey wasn't there to meet us. We missed him bumping against our legs as we walked up the sidewalk.

After dinner, the phone rang. It was Mrs. Johnson. "More cat trouble, I'm afraid," she said. "Humphrey has disappeared. He's probably on his way to your place."

"Is he?" I asked. What a clever cat, I thought.

"He should make it by tomorrow night," she said. "May I speak to your mom or dad?"

Dad went to the phone. There was a short pause before he said, "Yes, we'd love to keep him. Karl and Jenna have really missed him."

"Yay, yahoo!" I yelled and rushed out to tell Jenna. "He's coming home. Humphrey's coming home."

We jumped around, yelling, until Dad told us to be quiet. His lips had curled into a twitchy smile.

All the next day, I couldn't think about anything except Humphrey. I pictured him running along the sidewalk, heading for home – our home. He might even be waiting to meet us after school.

But Humphrey wasn't there. He still hadn't turned up at Jenna's bedtime. I put off going to bed for as long as possible, but he still wasn't there.

Sometimes, just before I go to sleep, I get scary little thoughts about things that might go wrong. That night I began worrying about Humphrey crossing the roads. "Don't be stupid," I told myself. "He's a sensible cat. He'll be fine."

But the next morning, Humphrey still hadn't come home.

By the end of that week I thought I had things pretty much under control – except at bedtime when I'd remember Humphrey looking down at us from the roof, or purring beside me as I went to sleep. Maybe I didn't have things under control after all.

But if I felt bad, Jenna felt much worse. She kept crying in the middle of the night, and Mom couldn't get her to eat her dinner.

"Perhaps we should take Mrs. Johnson's advice and get her a kitten," Mom said.

"Good idea," replied Dad. "Let's go to the animal shelter today."

Chapter 7

"It's the kitten season," the man at the animal shelter said. "Look at them all."

We stood beside him and stared at the cage of kittens. How were we ever going to choose?

Jenna had no trouble at all. "That one," she yelled, pointing to a fluffy ginger-and-white kitten. Its eyes were blue and its tail pointed straight up like an arrow. The man took it out of the cage and gave it to Jenna to cuddle.

"Mew, mew," it squeaked and dug its claws into her sweatshirt.

"You're so cute," Jenna said. "I'll call you Buttercup."

"What about you?" Mom asked me. "Do you like that one?"

I nodded and stroked its head with my finger. But I didn't care which kitten we took home. It just wasn't important to me.

"We have some older cats," the man said. "One or two nice strays. They're already house-trained. Would you like to see them?"

"I don't think so," Dad said.

"I'd like to see them," I said.

"What for?" Dad asked.

I shrugged. I didn't know why.

"OK, come this way," the man said. I followed while the others trailed after us.

And there was Humphrey, fast asleep. He slowly opened his eyes and rubbed against the bars of the cage and purred. It was as though he had expected us.

"That old thing was picked up at the end of your street just the other day. You don't want him," the man said. But I already had Humphrey out of his cage. He'd almost made it home, and I was going to take him the rest of the way.

"Yes we do," I said. "And he wants us!"

"Meow!" said Humphrey.

So we took two cats home. Humphrey and I don't think much of Buttercup. But I'm glad we've got her, because that means I have Humphrey all to myself.

From the Author

Most of us think cats belong to us – that cats are pets we choose to come and live with us and that we invite them to share our homes and our lives. But I don't think all cats see it that way. Humphrey surely doesn't. He's one of those cats who chooses his own people.

We went to live with a cat like that once. Like Humphrey, this cat refused to go with the family that lived there before us.

We worried about what would happen to him when we moved out. But everything turned out all right. We moved five houses down the street, and after a week, the cat moved, too.

Marie Gibson

From the Illustrator

I live in Palmerston North with my wife, Kim, and our three-year-old daughter, Tessa.

We also share our home with two ginger cats, Claude and Camille. Camille brought Claude home one day, and he decided to stay.

Cats can be quite a trial at times, especially in the middle of the night when you end up standing on a dead mouse that one of the cats has proudly brought inside. Or you discover the food that you put in the cupboard to thaw has disappeared.

But when you are sick or reading or, in my case, working late, a cat will always be near to keep you company.

Brent Putze

LITERACY TREE

Who Knows?

The Midnight Pig
PS I Love You, Gramps
Humphrey
Dinosaur Girl

The Dinosaur Connection
Myth or Mystery?
Hairy Little Critters
A Pocket Full of Posies

Written by **Marie Gibson**
Illustrated by **Brent Putze**

© 1999 Shortland Publications Inc.

05 04 03 02 01 00
10 9 8 7 6 5 4 3 2

Published in the United States by

Rigby
a division of Reed Elsevier Inc.
500 Coventry Lane
Crystal Lake, IL 60014

Printed in Hong Kong
ISBN: 0-7901-1876-9